GIRAFFES

by Lucia Raatma

Children's Press®

An Imprint of Scholastic Inc.
New York   Toronto   London   Auckland   Sydney
Mexico City   New Delhi   Hong Kong
Danbury, Connecticut

Content Consultant
Dr. Stephen S. Ditchkoff
Professor of Wildlife Sciences
Auburn University
Auburn, Alabama

Photographs © 2014: Alamy Images/blickwinkel: 19; AP Images/
Rex Features: 24; Dreamstime: 2, 3 background, 44, 45 background
(Annemario), 12 (Clearviewstock), 7 (Gbuglok), 15 (Ikachan),
1, 28, 46 (Znm); Getty Images: cover (Darrell Gulin), 27 (Suzi
Eszterhas), 40 (Tom Cockrem); Media Bakery/Sergio Pitamitz: 20;
Photo Researchers: 2 foreground, 5 top, 11 (Millard H. Sharp/
Science Source), 32 (Picture Partners/Science Source); Shutterstock,
Inc.: 4, 36 (Andrew F. Kazmierski), 35 (Kairos69), 16 (pakul54),
8 (PerseoMedusa); Superstock, Inc.: 23 (Animals Animals), 31
(DeAgostini), 5 bottom, 39 (Tips Images).

Library of Congress Cataloging-in-Publication Data
Raatma, Lucia.
 Giraffes / by Lucia Raatma.
 pages cm.—(Nature's children)
 Includes bibliographical references and index.
 Audience: Age 9–12.
 Audience: Grades 4–6.
 ISBN 978-0-531-23358-0 (lib. bdg.) — ISBN 978-0-531-25156-0
(pbk.)
 1. Giraffes—Juvenile literature. I. Title.
 QL737.U56R33 2013
 599.638—dc23   2013000280

Printed in China 62
SCHOLASTIC, CHILDREN'S PRESS, and associated logos are
trademarks and/or registered trademarks of Scholastic Inc.

2 3 4 5 6 7 8 9 10 R 23 22 21 20 19 18 17 16 15 14

Giraffes

Class	Mammalia
Order	Artiodactyla
Family	Giraffidae
Genus	*Giraffa*
Species	*Giraffa camelopardalis*
World distribution	Found in many African countries, including Kenya, Rwanda, South Africa, Uganda, Tanzania, and others
Habitat	Primarily found in savannas, woodlands, and grasslands
Distinctive physical characteristics	World's tallest land animals; very long necks; interesting coat patterns that help them blend into their surroundings
Habits	Usually live in groups of 6 to 20 animals; warn one another of danger; some are solitary; males use their necks and heads to fight one another and establish dominance
Diet	Mostly eat the leaves from acacia trees; also eat fruits, grasses, and twigs

GIRAFFES

Contents

CHAPTER 1

Heads in the Sky

Sunlight shines down on a beautiful afternoon in the African **savanna**. A warm breeze blows, rustling the grass that covers the vast open landscape. A huge variety of incredible animals roam the area, from zebras quietly munching on grass to elephants rumbling the ground with their heavy footsteps. Several lions nap together in the warm sun. But one **species** towers above all the rest. A small group of giraffes is munching on the leaves of a nearby acacia tree. Though the tree's branches are high above the ground, the giraffes have no problem reaching the tasty leaves.

Giraffes are amazing, long-necked animals that live throughout Africa. Their **habitat** is south of the Sahara Desert. It includes the African countries of Rwanda, Kenya, Uganda, South Africa, Tanzania, and many others. They live in grasslands, savannas, and woodlands.

Giraffes thrive in savannas, where a variety of wild grasses cover the ground and trees are scattered across the landscape.

Giraffe Basics

With their long legs and necks, giraffes are the tallest **mammals** found on land. Adults can reach heights of 14 to 19 feet (4.3 to 5.8 meters). That is taller than an average house! Male giraffes can weigh as much as 4,200 pounds (1,905 kilograms), while females can weigh up to 1,180 pounds (535 kg). A giraffe's neck alone weighs about 600 pounds (272 kg) and can be as long as 6 feet (1.8 m). That is taller than some adult humans.

Each of a giraffe's four long legs is about 6 feet (1.8 m) tall. It can appear as though the back legs are shorter than the front ones, but they are really the same length. In between a giraffe's long legs and neck, the main part of its body is actually quite short.

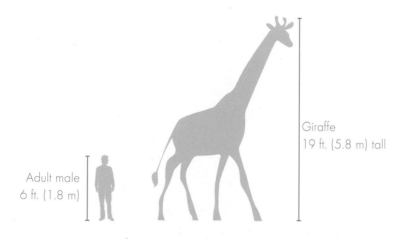

Adult male
6 ft. (1.8 m)

Giraffe
19 ft. (5.8 m) tall

A giraffe has such a long neck that it requires special blood vessels to pump blood all the way up to its head.

A Unique Appearance

There is only one species of giraffe. But there are several **subspecies.** The main difference among the various subspecies is their fur. Every giraffe has a unique pattern on its coat. No two giraffes have the exact same pattern. However, members of the same subspecies share similar types of colors and patterns.

For instance, the Rothschild's giraffe has large brown spots that are separated by lines of beige. It lives in Uganda and other areas. The Masai giraffe has spots that look like oak leaves. This giraffe lives in Kenya.

The reticulated giraffe lives in northern Kenya and southern Somalia. Its coat is dark with white lines that look like a spider's web. The Nubian giraffe is found in Ethiopia and Sudan. It has dark brown splotches with an off-white background. The West African giraffe lives in Nigeria. It has a very light-colored coat with rectangular-shaped spots. A giraffe's coat provides the animal with **camouflage,** helping it blend in with its surroundings.

A reticulated giraffe's fur is mostly brown.

Bumps and Bones

A giraffe's head has two big ears that stick up or out to the sides. It also has two long bumps that look like horns. These structures are really just **cartilage** that is covered with hair. They are called ossicones. The ossicones on females are thin and have more hair. The ossicones on males are usually thicker and can become bald over time.

Male giraffes sometimes use their ossicones to fight one another. As they get older, their skulls change shapes based on where they have hit them against other giraffes' heads. Areas of **calcium** build up in these areas to help protect the giraffes as they fight. These lumpy spots can look like extra horns.

Giraffes have very long necks, but each has just seven **vertebrae**. That is the same number of vertebrae that humans have in their necks. However, a giraffe's vertebrae may each be as long as 10 inches (25.4 centimeters).

As male giraffes fight one another, their ossicones rub together, sometimes causing the hair to fall out.

CHAPTER 2

Surviving the African Wilds

There are many wild animals in Africa. Many of them are fierce hunters. Lions, crocodiles, leopards, and hyenas can all pose a threat to giraffes. To protect themselves, giraffes usually live in small groups of 6 to 20 animals and watch out for one another. The giraffes' height helps them see **predators** coming from far away.

If giraffes are attacked, they fight back with a quick kick from their powerful legs. They can also run as fast as 37 miles per hour (60 kilometers per hour) to escape danger.

Male giraffes often battle each other to prove their **dominance**. The giraffes fight with their heads and necks. When "necking," they may rub their necks against each other or swing them to land powerful blows on the opponent. In rare situations, a giraffe can be hurt or killed in one of these fights. After most battles, however, the losing giraffe just walks away.

Giraffes fight each other using their heads and necks.

Eating All the Time

Giraffes are **herbivores**. This means they eat plants. Their favorite food is the leaves of acacia trees. They can eat only a few leaves with each bite. This means they must spend many hours every day eating. A single giraffe eats as much as 75 pounds (34 kg) of leaves in a day.

Acacia trees have thorns, but giraffes use their long, narrow tongue and **prehensile** lips to eat around them. If they accidentally chew on a thorn, their thick **saliva** helps protect their mouth. Giraffes also eat grasses, fruits, twigs, and other leaves.

Giraffes are **ruminants**. This means they have stomachs with four sections. After they eat, they chew their **cud**. This is a process in which after the giraffes swallow a batch of leaves, it comes back up their throats. They chew and grind it some more. Then they swallow the food again.

A giraffe's long tongue has tough outer layers that protect it from thorns and other sharp points as it twists between tree branches.

Dangers for Giraffes

Giraffes spend much of their time watching for surprise attacks as they eat. Lions can strike suddenly, and crocodiles can grab giraffes at watering holes. No matter where they are, giraffes are always careful. They have to be prepared for any danger. Giraffes also know that their **calves** are not as big and strong as adults. Hyenas and leopards sometimes **prey** upon giraffe calves, so mother giraffes have to watch over their young carefully.

In addition to wild animals, giraffes face other threats. Many people hunt them for their meat and skins. In addition, there is less room for giraffes and other wildlife to live as the human population in Africa grows. Giraffes lose their habitat when grasslands are cleared for villages. They also lose their habitat when roads are built. Trees are cut down, and natural areas change. This makes it harder for the giraffes to find food.

Lions are ferocious hunters that roam the African savanna in search of giraffes and other prey.

Long-Necked Lookouts

There is a lot of water in the leaves that giraffes eat, so they do not need to drink water often. They have to drink more often during dry seasons. When giraffes drink water, they must spread their legs out wide so their long necks can reach down. When giraffes are bent over like this, crocodiles can attack them. Usually, giraffes go to watering holes in groups. This allows one giraffe to stand watch while the others drink.

Giraffes do not need much sleep. Most giraffes sleep off and on during the night. Some giraffes take short one- to two-minute naps throughout the day. A giraffe might sleep standing up, or it might lie down with its head resting on its body. However, a giraffe is more likely to be attacked by lions when it lies down. To prevent this from happening, giraffes often take turns standing guard while others sleep.

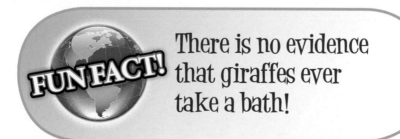

FUN FACT! There is no evidence that giraffes ever take a bath!

A giraffe's unique body shape leaves the animal vulnerable to attacks when it bends over to drink.

CHAPTER 3

A Giraffe's Life

Giraffes often live in groups. But they do not stay with the same group their whole lives. The groups change frequently as old members leave and new ones arrive. The most common groups are made up of females and their calves. Young males often form groups where they can practice fighting with one another. Older males sometimes drift off from groups and are more **solitary**.

Giraffes communicate using a wide range of sounds. Calves may use mooing and mewing noises. Mothers may bellow to call their young. During **mating** season, males often make coughing sounds. When in danger, giraffes can make snorting noises to warn the others. Giraffes also hiss, roar, and grunt. Scientists believe that giraffes use **infrasound** to communicate over long distances. Humans cannot hear infrasound because it is an extremely low sound.

While giraffes are rarely heard by humans, they are capable of making many different sounds.

Big Babies

After a male and a female mate, the mother giraffe is pregnant for about 14 to 15 months. When it is time for a giraffe mother to give birth, she often returns to the place where she was born. The mother stands as she gives birth to her calf. A baby giraffe is born feetfirst, dropping from its mother to the ground. It may drop as far as 6.6 feet (2 m), but it does not get hurt. The calf can walk within the first hour of its life. Within a few hours, it can run with its mother.

Usually, only one calf is born at a time. But sometimes a mother will have two calves at once. A baby giraffe is about 6 feet (1.8 m) tall and weighs 100 to 150 pounds (45 to 68 kg) at birth. Within a year, the calf will nearly double in height.

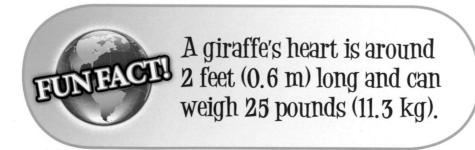

FUN FACT! A giraffe's heart is around 2 feet (0.6 m) long and can weigh 25 pounds (11.3 kg).

Mother giraffes can be very affectionate, sometimes nuzzling and licking their calves.

Growing Up

Baby giraffes drink their mother's milk when they are first born. When they are around 4 months old, the calves start feeding on leaves. At this point, they learn to chew their cud. Most continue to drink their mother's milk along with their leafy meals until they are 9 to 12 months old.

During the first week of a calf's life, a mother may hide her baby in the tall grass and leave it alone while she goes out to eat leaves. The calf stays quiet and waits for its mother's return.

Mothers and calves often join other giraffe families to form a group that is like a nursery. In the group, the calves play with one another. One mother will watch all the calves while the other mothers go out to feed. Hyenas, lions, and wild dogs are a threat to baby giraffes, so the mothers are very protective of their young.

Young giraffes are very energetic, and they love to run and play.

The Life Cycle

Male calves usually stay with their mothers for about 15 months. Then they leave to join groups with other males. Female calves stay with their mothers for about 18 months. In most cases, they stay close to the area where they were born, even after leaving their mothers. When they are between three and five years old, the young giraffes begin mating. Then they will have calves of their own.

Scientists believe that nearly 50 percent of giraffe calves do not survive their first six months. But once they grow up, giraffes are better able to protect themselves and help keep their group safe. Most giraffes live to be about 20 to 25 years old in the wild. This varies depending on what region of Africa they live in. Giraffes that live in zoos and other protected areas can live even longer.

FUN FACT! A giraffe's heart can beat up to 170 times a minute.

Young giraffes stay under the watchful protection of their nursery groups until they are strong enough to strike out on their own.

CHAPTER 4

Yesterday and Today

Giraffes have small humps on their backs. They also have spotted patterns on their coats. For these reasons, ancient Greek and Roman people thought giraffes were a combination of camels and leopards. That is why the animal's species name is *camelopardalis*. Some Roman people enjoyed collecting animals. According to one story, ruler Julius Caesar brought a giraffe to Rome in 46 BCE and showed it off to the people of the city.

Scientists have discovered fossils of giraffes in India, China, Japan, Africa, and other areas. They believe that giraffes lived more than 20 million years ago. The fossils show that the animals were tall and had ossicones. Some fossils show that ancient giraffes had short necks. The species changed over time, and their necks got longer.

Drawings of giraffes have been discovered on rocks in the Sahara Desert.

A Giraffe's Relative

Today, the giraffe's only close relative is the okapi. The okapi lives in the central part of Africa. It has black and white stripes on parts of its body. This pattern helps it blend into its surroundings. Some people think the okapi resembles a zebra. However, it is actually much more similar to a giraffe. The okapi has big ears that stand up. It has ossicones on its head. It also has a long prehensile tongue that helps it eat leaves.

The okapi is not as tall as a giraffe, though. It is only about 5 feet (1.5 m) high. This height is better suited for the rain forest where the okapi lives. In the rain forest, tree branches hang down low. Being as tall as a giraffe would make it hard for an okapi to get around.

An adult okapi weighs up to about 660 pounds (300 kg).

Living with Humans

Giraffes have been a part of people's lives for thousands of years. There are many African folktales about why the giraffe is so tall. Throughout Africa, giraffes are shown on rocks and in ancient cave drawings. In Tanzania, the giraffe is the national animal.

Long ago, people in Egypt often treated giraffes as pets. In the 1400s, giraffes were shipped from Egypt to China and Europe. They were given as gifts to important leaders and royalty. People were amazed by the strange appearance of these animals.

Throughout the world, giraffes have been main characters in children's books and movies. They are often shown in paintings. For many people, the giraffe is a favorite animal to visit at the zoo. Even a constellation called Camelopardalis is named for the long-necked animal.

Zoos and wildlife parks let people come face-to-face with giraffes.

CHAPTER 5

What's in Store?

Two types of giraffes are considered endangered. This means they are at risk of dying out forever. These two subspecies are the West African giraffe and the Rothschild's giraffe. By some estimates, fewer than 250 West African giraffes and fewer than 670 Rothschild's giraffes live in the wild. Other types of giraffes are not at such risk. However, the total giraffe population is much smaller than it once was. According to one conservation group, there were more than 140,000 giraffes in 1999. In recent years, that number has dropped below 80,000.

The biggest danger for giraffes is loss of habitat. As the human population grows, so do the towns and cities where they live. As natural areas are cleared and changed into villages and roads, the grasslands disappear. Giraffes have less space to feed, mate, and raise their young.

Giraffes are forced to share their living space with people.

Hunting Giraffes

For thousands of years, the people of Africa hunted giraffes. They ate the giraffe meat and used hair from giraffe tails for thread, brushes, and jewelry. They used giraffe skin for shoes and drums, and made musical instruments from the animal's body parts. In the 1800s, people began hunting giraffes as a sport.

Today, people still hunt giraffes when they go on African safaris. Hunters travel to Africa from all over the world. They pay guides to take them hunting. They take pride in killing giraffes and making trophies out of them. This practice is legal for giraffes that are not considered endangered. Some people believe that all giraffes should be protected. Others feel people have a right to hunt these animals, just as they would hunt deer or birds. They also argue that these hunting trips bring in much-needed money to African countries.

FUN FACT! A giraffe's tongue often reaches 20 inches (50.8 cm) in length.

Safari groups travel into the wilderness to hunt for wild animals such as giraffes.

Protecting Giraffes

There are groups that are working to protect giraffes. The Giraffe Conservation Foundation promotes the importance of giraffes and tries to protect their habitat. This group also looks for threats to giraffes and finds ways to end those threats.

In Kenya, Giraffe Manor is a hotel that is home to a number of endangered Rothschild's giraffes. This hotel protects the giraffes and helps them have calves. Throughout Africa, there are also wildlife **preserves** and national parks where giraffes are kept safe.

In countries all over the globe, many giraffes live in zoos and wildlife parks. There, they are protected and cared for. At zoos and parks, visitors can see giraffes up close. They can also learn why these remarkable animals are so special to the world.

Giraffe Manor has a hotel where giraffes are allowed to roam the area and visit with guests.

Words to Know

calcium (KAL-see-uhm) — a silver-white element found in teeth and bones

calves (KAVZ) — the young of several large species of animals, such as giraffes, cows, seals, elephants, and whales

camouflage (KAM-uh-flahzh) — a disguise or a natural coloring that allows animals, people, or objects to hide by making them look like their surroundings

cartilage (KAHR-ti-lij) — a strong, elastic tissue that forms the outer ear and nose of humans and mammals, and lines the bones at the joints

conservation (kahn-sur-VAY-shuhn) — the protection of valuable things, especially forests, wildlife, natural resources, or artistic or historic objects

cud (KUHD) — food that some animals, such as cows and sheep, bring up from the first part of their stomachs to chew again

dominance (DAH-muh-nuntz) — the power of one animal or person to assert its will over another

endangered (en-DAYN-jurd) — at risk of becoming extinct, usually because of human activity

fossils (FAH-suhlz) — bones, shells, or other traces of an animal or plant from long ago, preserved as rock

habitat (HAB-uh-tat) — the place where an animal or a plant naturally lives

herbivores (HUR-buh-vorz) — animals that eat only plants

infrasound (IN-frah-sound) — a type of sound wave that is below the levels that humans can hear

mammals (MAM-uhlz) — warm-blooded animals that have hair or fur and usually give birth to live babies; female mammals produce milk to feed their young

mating (MAYT-ing) — joining together to produce babies

predators (PRED-uh-turz) — animals that live by hunting other animals for food

prehensile (pree-HEN-sile) — adapted for seizing or grasping especially by wrapping around

preserves (pri-ZURVZ) — places where plants and animals are protected in their natural environment

prey (PRAY) — to hunt and eat another animal; an animal that is hunted by another animal for food

ruminants (ROO-muh-nuhnts) — animals that have four-chambered stomachs and chew cud

safaris (suh-FAHR-eez) — trips taken, usually to Africa, to see or hunt large, wild animals

saliva (suh-LYE-vuh) — the watery fluid in an animal's mouth that keeps it moist and helps the animal soften and swallow food

savanna (suh-VAN-uh) — a flat, grassy plain with few or no trees; savannas are found in tropical and subtropical areas

solitary (SAHL-uh-ter-ee) — not requiring or without the companionship of others

species (SPEE-sheez) — one of the groups into which animals and plants of the same genus are divided; members of the same species can mate and have offspring

subspecies (SUHB-spee-sheez) — a category in biological classification that ranks immediately below a species and includes a physically recognizable and geographically separate group; members of different subspecies of the same species can mate and have offspring

vertebrae (VUR-tuh-bray) — small bones that make up the backbone of an animal

Habitat Map

NORTH

AMERICA

PACIFIC

OCEAN

ATLANTIC

SOUTH
AMERICA

Giraffe Range

ARCTIC OCEAN

EUROPE

ASIA

AFRICA

PACIFIC
OCEAN

OCEAN

INDIAN
OCEAN

AUSTRALIA

Find Out More

Books
Friedman, Mel. *Africa*. New York: Children's Press, 2009.

Helget, Nicole. *Giraffes*. Mankato, MN: Creative Education, 2009.

Stewart, Melissa. *Giraffe Graphs*. New York: Children's Press, 2007.

Visit this Scholastic Web site for more information on giraffes:
www.factsfornow.scholastic.com
Enter the keyword **Giraffes**

Index

Page numbers in *italics* indicate a photograph or map.

About the Author

Lucia Raatma earned a bachelor's degree from the University of South Carolina and a master's degree from New York University. She has authored dozens of books for young readers, and she particularly enjoys writing about wildlife and conservation. She and her family love getting the chance to feed giraffes at the local zoo.